THIS BOOK BELONGS TO:

CONTACT INFORMATION

NAME:

ADDRESS:

PHONE:

START / END DATES

/   /   TO   /   /

DEDICATION

This Beer Review Log Book is dedicated to all the beer enthusiasts out there who want to record their beer tastings and document their findings in the process.

You are my inspiration for producing books and I'm honored to be a part of keeping all of your beer review notes and records organized.

This journal notebook will help you record the details of your beer tasting adventures.

Thoughtfully put together with these sections to record: Beer Name, Brewery, Tasting Date, Style, Alcohol by Volume, Bottled by, Price, Container, Appearance, Clarity, Sediment, Aroma, Taste, Palate, Notes, Summary, Favorite Brews, and much more!

HOW TO USE THIS BOOK

The purpose of this book is to keep all of your beer review notes all in one place. It will help keep you organized.

This Beer Review Log Book will allow you to accurately document every detail about sending your beer tasting advetures.

Here are examples of the prompts for you to fill in and write about your experience in this book:

1. Beer Name - Write the name of the beer.
2. Brewery - Record the name of the brewer.
3. Tasting Date - Log the date you tasted.
4. Style - Write the style of the beer.
5. Alcohol By Volume - Record the alcohol percentage.
6. Bottled By - Log which company bottled it.
7. Price - Write the price.
8. Container - Is it a bottle, can, draft, growler, cask, or other.
9. Appearance - Is it golden, amber, copper, red, brown, black or other.
10. Clarity - Is it crystal, clear, hazy, opaque, or other.
11. Head Size, Retentions, and Description - Record the head size, retention & description.
12. Sediment - Is there some, none, or tons.
13. Aroma - Record what it smells like. Does it smell malty, roasty, hoppy, earthy, fruity, sour, spicy, or smoky.
14. Taste Is it tart, sweet, bitter, or boozy.
15. Palate - How does it feel in your mouth. Is it light-bodied, medium-bodied, full-bodied, or effervescent.
16. Notes - Plenty of blank lined space for writing any important details such as first impressions, favorite recipes with the brews, favorite brewing company,
17. Comparisons - Write any comparisons
18. Food Pairings - Record what food you tried with it and if it was a good pairing.
19. Recommend? - Yes or no.
20. Overall Rating - Rate the taste from 1-10.
21. Summary - Write a summary of your tasting.
22. Favorite Brews - Space to record your favorite brews including Beer name, Brewery, Date, and Style.

BEER TASTING NOTES

BEER NAME

BREWERY

TASTING DATE: **STYLE**

ALCOHOL BY VOLUME: **BOTTLED BY / BEST BY** **PRICE**

CONTAINER
- ☐ BOTTLE
- ☐ CAN
- ☐ DRAFT
- ☐ GROWLER
- ☐ CASK
- ☐ OTHER

APPEARANCE
- ☐ GOLDEN
- ☐ AMBER
- ☐ COPPER
- ☐ RED
- ☐ BROWN
- ☐ BLACK
- ☐ OTHER

CLARITY
- ☐ CRYSTAL
- ☐ CLEAR
- ☐ HAZY
- ☐ OPAQUE
- ☐ OTHER

HEAD SIZE

HEAD RETENTION

HEAD DESCRIPTION
- ☐ SPARSE
- ☐ OTHER
- ☐ LIGHT
- ☐ CREAMY
- ☐ SOAPY
- ☐ FROTHY

SEDIMENT
- ☐ NONE
- ☐ SOME
- ☐ TONS

AROMA
- ☐ MALTY
- ☐ ROASTY
- ☐ HOPPY
- ☐ EARTHY
- ☐ FRUITY
- ☐ SOUR
- ☐ SPICY
- ☐ SMOKEY

NOTES

TASTE
- ☐ TART
- ☐ BITTER
- ☐ SWEET
- ☐ BOOZY

NOTES

PALATE (THE WAY THE BEER FEELS IN YOUR MOUTH)
- ☐ LIGHT-BODIED (THIN + WATERY)
- ☐ MEDIUM-BODIED (LIGHT + FULL)
- ☐ FULL-BODIED (RICH + CREAMY)
- ☐ EFFERVESCENT

NOTES

BEER TASTING NOTES

COMPARISONS

FOOD/MEAL PAIRINGS

SHARED WITH (FAMILY/FRIENDS)

RECOMMEND?
☐ YES ☐ NO

RATING
☐ 1 ☐ 2 ☐ 3 ☐ 4 ☐ 5 ☐ 6 ☐ 7 ☐ 8 ☐ 9 ☐ 10

SUMMARY

BEER TASTING NOTES

BEER NAME

BREWERY

TASTING DATE: **STYLE**

ALCOHOL BY VOLUME: **BOTTLED BY / BEST BY** **PRICE**

CONTAINER
- ☐ BOTTLE
- ☐ CAN
- ☐ DRAFT
- ☐ GROWLER
- ☐ CASK
- ☐ OTHER

APPEARANCE
- ☐ GOLDEN
- ☐ AMBER
- ☐ COPPER
- ☐ RED
- ☐ BROWN
- ☐ BLACK
- ☐ OTHER

CLARITY
- ☐ CRYSTAL
- ☐ CLEAR
- ☐ HAZY
- ☐ OPAQUE
- ☐ OTHER

HEAD SIZE

HEAD RETENTION

HEAD DESCRIPTION
- ☐ SPARSE   ☐ OTHER
- ☐ LIGHT
- ☐ CREAMY
- ☐ SOAPY
- ☐ FROTHY

SEDIMENT
- ☐ NONE
- ☐ SOME
- ☐ TONS

AROMA
- ☐ MALTY
- ☐ ROASTY
- ☐ HOPPY
- ☐ EARTHY
- ☐ FRUITY
- ☐ SOUR
- ☐ SPICY
- ☐ SMOKEY

NOTES

TASTE
- ☐ TART
- ☐ BITTER
- ☐ SWEET
- ☐ BOOZY

NOTES

PALATE (THE WAY THE BEER FEELS IN YOUR MOUTH)
- ☐ LIGHT-BODIED (THIN + WATERY)
- ☐ MEDIUM-BODIED (LIGHT + FULL)
- ☐ FULL-BODIED (RICH + CREAMY)
- ☐ EFFERVESCENT

NOTES

BEER TASTING NOTES

COMPARISONS

FOOD/MEAL PAIRINGS

SHARED WITH (FAMILY/FRIENDS)

RECOMMEND? | RATING
☐ YES   ☐ NO | ☐ 1   ☐ 2   ☐ 3   ☐ 4   ☐ 5   ☐ 6   ☐ 7   ☐ 8   ☐ 9   ☐ 10

SUMMARY

BEER TASTING NOTES

BEER NAME

BREWERY

TASTING DATE: **STYLE**

ALCOHOL BY VOLUME: **BOTTLED BY / BEST BY** **PRICE**

CONTAINER
- ☐ BOTTLE
- ☐ CAN
- ☐ DRAFT
- ☐ GROWLER
- ☐ CASK
- ☐ OTHER

APPEARANCE
- ☐ GOLDEN
- ☐ AMBER
- ☐ COPPER
- ☐ RED
- ☐ BROWN
- ☐ BLACK
- ☐ OTHER

CLARITY
- ☐ CRYSTAL
- ☐ CLEAR
- ☐ HAZY
- ☐ OPAQUE
- ☐ OTHER

HEAD SIZE

HEAD RETENTION

HEAD DESCRIPTION
- ☐ SPARSE
- ☐ LIGHT
- ☐ CREAMY
- ☐ SOAPY
- ☐ FROTHY
- ☐ OTHER

SEDIMENT
- ☐ NONE
- ☐ SOME
- ☐ TONS

AROMA
- ☐ MALTY
- ☐ ROASTY
- ☐ HOPPY
- ☐ EARTHY
- ☐ FRUITY
- ☐ SOUR
- ☐ SPICY
- ☐ SMOKEY

NOTES

TASTE
- ☐ TART
- ☐ BITTER
- ☐ SWEET
- ☐ BOOZY

NOTES

PALATE (THE WAY THE BEER FEELS IN YOUR MOUTH)
- ☐ LIGHT-BODIED (THIN + WATERY)
- ☐ MEDIUM-BODIED (LIGHT + FULL)
- ☐ FULL-BODIED (RICH + CREAMY)
- ☐ EFFERVESCENT

NOTES

BEER TASTING NOTES

COMPARISONS

FOOD/MEAL PAIRINGS

SHARED WITH (FAMILY/FRIENDS)

RECOMMEND?
☐ YES   ☐ NO

RATING
☐ 1   ☐ 2   ☐ 3   ☐ 4   ☐ 5   ☐ 6   ☐ 7   ☐ 8   ☐ 9   ☐ 10

SUMMARY

BEER TASTING NOTES

BEER NAME

BREWERY

TASTING DATE: **STYLE**

ALCOHOL BY VOLUME: **BOTTLED BY / BEST BY** **PRICE**

CONTAINER
- ☐ BOTTLE
- ☐ CAN
- ☐ DRAFT
- ☐ GROWLER
- ☐ CASK
- ☐ OTHER

APPEARANCE
- ☐ GOLDEN
- ☐ AMBER
- ☐ COPPER
- ☐ RED
- ☐ BROWN
- ☐ BLACK
- ☐ OTHER

CLARITY
- ☐ CRYSTAL
- ☐ CLEAR
- ☐ HAZY
- ☐ OPAQUE
- ☐ OTHER

HEAD SIZE

HEAD RETENTION

HEAD DESCRIPTION
- ☐ SPARSE   ☐ OTHER
- ☐ LIGHT
- ☐ CREAMY
- ☐ SOAPY
- ☐ FROTHY

SEDIMENT
- ☐ NONE
- ☐ SOME
- ☐ TONS

AROMA
- ☐ MALTY
- ☐ ROASTY
- ☐ HOPPY
- ☐ EARTHY
- ☐ FRUITY
- ☐ SOUR
- ☐ SPICY
- ☐ SMOKEY

NOTES

TASTE
- ☐ TART
- ☐ BITTER
- ☐ SWEET
- ☐ BOOZY

NOTES

PALATE (THE WAY THE BEER FEELS IN YOUR MOUTH)
- ☐ LIGHT-BODIED (THIN + WATERY)
- ☐ MEDIUM-BODIED (LIGHT + FULL)
- ☐ FULL-BODIED (RICH + CREAMY)
- ☐ EFFERVESCENT

NOTES

BEER TASTING NOTES

COMPARISONS

FOOD/MEAL PAIRINGS

SHARED WITH (FAMILY/FRIENDS)

RECOMMEND?
☐ YES ☐ NO

RATING
☐ 1 ☐ 2 ☐ 3 ☐ 4 ☐ 5 ☐ 6 ☐ 7 ☐ 8 ☐ 9 ☐ 10

SUMMARY

BEER TASTING NOTES

BEER NAME

BREWERY

TASTING DATE: **STYLE**

ALCOHOL BY VOLUME: **BOTTLED BY / BEST BY** **PRICE**

CONTAINER
- ☐ BOTTLE
- ☐ CAN
- ☐ DRAFT
- ☐ GROWLER
- ☐ CASK
- ☐ OTHER

APPEARANCE
- ☐ GOLDEN
- ☐ AMBER
- ☐ COPPER
- ☐ RED
- ☐ BROWN
- ☐ BLACK
- ☐ OTHER

CLARITY
- ☐ CRYSTAL
- ☐ CLEAR
- ☐ HAZY
- ☐ OPAQUE
- ☐ OTHER

HEAD SIZE

HEAD RETENTION

HEAD DESCRIPTION
- ☐ SPARSE   ☐ OTHER
- ☐ LIGHT
- ☐ CREAMY
- ☐ SOAPY
- ☐ FROTHY

SEDIMENT
- ☐ NONE
- ☐ SOME
- ☐ TONS

AROMA
- ☐ MALTY
- ☐ ROASTY
- ☐ HOPPY
- ☐ EARTHY
- ☐ FRUITY
- ☐ SOUR
- ☐ SPICY
- ☐ SMOKEY

NOTES

TASTE
- ☐ TART
- ☐ BITTER
- ☐ SWEET
- ☐ BOOZY

NOTES

PALATE (THE WAY THE BEER FEELS IN YOUR MOUTH)
- ☐ LIGHT-BODIED (THIN + WATERY)
- ☐ MEDIUM-BODIED (LIGHT + FULL)
- ☐ FULL-BODIED (RICH + CREAMY)
- ☐ EFFERVESCENT

NOTES

BEER TASTING NOTES

COMPARISONS

FOOD/MEAL PAIRINGS

SHARED WITH (FAMILY/FRIENDS)

RECOMMEND?
☐ YES ☐ NO

RATING
☐ 1 ☐ 2 ☐ 3 ☐ 4 ☐ 5 ☐ 6 ☐ 7 ☐ 8 ☐ 9 ☐ 10

SUMMARY

BEER TASTING NOTES

BEER NAME

BREWERY

TASTING DATE: STYLE

ALCOHOL BY VOLUME: BOTTLED BY / BEST BY PRICE

CONTAINER
- ☐ BOTTLE
- ☐ CAN
- ☐ DRAFT
- ☐ GROWLER
- ☐ CASK
- ☐ OTHER

APPEARANCE
- ☐ GOLDEN
- ☐ AMBER
- ☐ COPPER
- ☐ RED
- ☐ BROWN
- ☐ BLACK
- ☐ OTHER

CLARITY
- ☐ CRYSTAL
- ☐ CLEAR
- ☐ HAZY
- ☐ OPAQUE
- ☐ OTHER

HEAD SIZE

HEAD RETENTION

HEAD DESCRIPTION
- ☐ SPARSE
- ☐ LIGHT
- ☐ CREAMY
- ☐ SOAPY
- ☐ FROTHY
- ☐ OTHER

SEDIMENT
- ☐ NONE
- ☐ SOME
- ☐ TONS

AROMA
- ☐ MALTY
- ☐ ROASTY
- ☐ HOPPY
- ☐ EARTHY
- ☐ FRUITY
- ☐ SOUR
- ☐ SPICY
- ☐ SMOKEY

NOTES

TASTE
- ☐ TART
- ☐ BITTER
- ☐ SWEET
- ☐ BOOZY

NOTES

PALATE (THE WAY THE BEER FEELS IN YOUR MOUTH)
- ☐ LIGHT-BODIED (THIN + WATERY)
- ☐ MEDIUM-BODIED (LIGHT + FULL)
- ☐ FULL-BODIED (RICH + CREAMY)
- ☐ EFFERVESCENT

NOTES

BEER TASTING NOTES

COMPARISONS

FOOD/MEAL PAIRINGS

SHARED WITH (FAMILY/FRIENDS)

RECOMMEND?
☐ YES ☐ NO

RATING
☐ 1 ☐ 2 ☐ 3 ☐ 4 ☐ 5 ☐ 6 ☐ 7 ☐ 8 ☐ 9 ☐ 10

SUMMARY

BEER TASTING NOTES

BEER NAME

BREWERY

TASTING DATE: **STYLE**

ALCOHOL BY VOLUME: **BOTTLED BY / BEST BY** **PRICE**

CONTAINER
- ☐ BOTTLE
- ☐ CAN
- ☐ DRAFT
- ☐ GROWLER
- ☐ CASK
- ☐ OTHER

APPEARANCE
- ☐ GOLDEN
- ☐ AMBER
- ☐ COPPER
- ☐ RED
- ☐ BROWN
- ☐ BLACK
- ☐ OTHER

CLARITY
- ☐ CRYSTAL
- ☐ CLEAR
- ☐ HAZY
- ☐ OPAQUE
- ☐ OTHER

HEAD SIZE

HEAD RETENTION

HEAD DESCRIPTION
- ☐ SPARSE
- ☐ LIGHT
- ☐ CREAMY
- ☐ SOAPY
- ☐ FROTHY
- ☐ OTHER

SEDIMENT
- ☐ NONE
- ☐ SOME
- ☐ TONS

AROMA
- ☐ MALTY
- ☐ ROASTY
- ☐ HOPPY
- ☐ EARTHY
- ☐ FRUITY
- ☐ SOUR
- ☐ SPICY
- ☐ SMOKEY

NOTES

TASTE
- ☐ TART
- ☐ BITTER
- ☐ SWEET
- ☐ BOOZY

NOTES

PALATE (THE WAY THE BEER FEELS IN YOUR MOUTH)
- ☐ LIGHT-BODIED (THIN + WATERY)
- ☐ MEDIUM-BODIED (LIGHT + FULL)
- ☐ FULL-BODIED (RICH + CREAMY)
- ☐ EFFERVESCENT

NOTES

BEER TASTING NOTES

COMPARISONS

FOOD/MEAL PAIRINGS

SHARED WITH (FAMILY/FRIENDS)

RECOMMEND?
☐ YES ☐ NO

RATING
☐ 1 ☐ 2 ☐ 3 ☐ 4 ☐ 5 ☐ 6 ☐ 7 ☐ 8 ☐ 9 ☐ 10

SUMMARY

BEER TASTING NOTES

BEER NAME

BREWERY

TASTING DATE: **STYLE**

ALCOHOL BY VOLUME: **BOTTLED BY / BEST BY**   **PRICE**

CONTAINER
- ☐ BOTTLE
- ☐ CAN
- ☐ DRAFT
- ☐ GROWLER
- ☐ CASK
- ☐ OTHER

APPEARANCE
- ☐ GOLDEN
- ☐ AMBER
- ☐ COPPER
- ☐ RED
- ☐ BROWN
- ☐ BLACK
- ☐ OTHER

CLARITY
- ☐ CRYSTAL
- ☐ CLEAR
- ☐ HAZY
- ☐ OPAQUE
- ☐ OTHER

HEAD SIZE

HEAD RETENTION

HEAD DESCRIPTION
- ☐ SPARSE   ☐ OTHER
- ☐ LIGHT
- ☐ CREAMY
- ☐ SOAPY
- ☐ FROTHY

SEDIMENT
- ☐ NONE
- ☐ SOME
- ☐ TONS

AROMA
- ☐ MALTY
- ☐ ROASTY
- ☐ HOPPY
- ☐ EARTHY
- ☐ FRUITY
- ☐ SOUR
- ☐ SPICY
- ☐ SMOKEY

NOTES

TASTE
- ☐ TART
- ☐ BITTER
- ☐ SWEET
- ☐ BOOZY

NOTES

PALATE (THE WAY THE BEER FEELS IN YOUR MOUTH)
- ☐ LIGHT-BODIED (THIN + WATERY)
- ☐ MEDIUM-BODIED (LIGHT + FULL)
- ☐ FULL-BODIED (RICH + CREAMY)
- ☐ EFFERVESCENT

NOTES

BEER TASTING NOTES

COMPARISONS

FOOD/MEAL PAIRINGS

SHARED WITH (FAMILY/FRIENDS)

RECOMMEND?　　☐ YES　　☐ NO

RATING　☐ 1　☐ 2　☐ 3　☐ 4　☐ 5　☐ 6　☐ 7　☐ 8　☐ 9　☐ 10

SUMMARY

BEER TASTING NOTES

BEER NAME

BREWERY

TASTING DATE: **STYLE**

ALCOHOL BY VOLUME: **BOTTLED BY / BEST BY**   **PRICE**

CONTAINER
- ☐ BOTTLE
- ☐ CAN
- ☐ DRAFT
- ☐ GROWLER
- ☐ CASK
- ☐ OTHER

APPEARANCE
- ☐ GOLDEN
- ☐ AMBER
- ☐ COPPER
- ☐ RED
- ☐ BROWN
- ☐ BLACK
- ☐ OTHER

CLARITY
- ☐ CRYSTAL
- ☐ CLEAR
- ☐ HAZY
- ☐ OPAQUE
- ☐ OTHER

HEAD SIZE

HEAD RETENTION

HEAD DESCRIPTION
- ☐ SPARSE
- ☐ LIGHT
- ☐ CREAMY
- ☐ SOAPY
- ☐ FROTHY
- ☐ OTHER

SEDIMENT
- ☐ NONE
- ☐ SOME
- ☐ TONS

AROMA
- ☐ MALTY
- ☐ ROASTY
- ☐ HOPPY
- ☐ EARTHY
- ☐ FRUITY
- ☐ SOUR
- ☐ SPICY
- ☐ SMOKEY

NOTES

TASTE
- ☐ TART
- ☐ BITTER
- ☐ SWEET
- ☐ BOOZY

NOTES

PALATE (THE WAY THE BEER FEELS IN YOUR MOUTH)
- ☐ LIGHT-BODIED (THIN + WATERY)
- ☐ MEDIUM-BODIED (LIGHT + FULL)
- ☐ FULL-BODIED (RICH + CREAMY)
- ☐ EFFERVESCENT

NOTES

BEER TASTING NOTES

COMPARISONS

FOOD/MEAL PAIRINGS

SHARED WITH (FAMILY/FRIENDS)

RECOMMEND? ☐ YES ☐ NO

RATING ☐ 1 ☐ 2 ☐ 3 ☐ 4 ☐ 5 ☐ 6 ☐ 7 ☐ 8 ☐ 9 ☐ 10

SUMMARY

BEER TASTING NOTES

BEER NAME

BREWERY

TASTING DATE: **STYLE**

ALCOHOL BY VOLUME: **BOTTLED BY / BEST BY** **PRICE**

CONTAINER
- ☐ BOTTLE
- ☐ CAN
- ☐ DRAFT
- ☐ GROWLER
- ☐ CASK
- ☐ OTHER

APPEARANCE
- ☐ GOLDEN
- ☐ AMBER
- ☐ COPPER
- ☐ RED
- ☐ BROWN
- ☐ BLACK
- ☐ OTHER

CLARITY
- ☐ CRYSTAL
- ☐ CLEAR
- ☐ HAZY
- ☐ OPAQUE
- ☐ OTHER

HEAD SIZE

HEAD RETENTION

HEAD DESCRIPTION
- ☐ SPARSE
- ☐ LIGHT
- ☐ CREAMY
- ☐ SOAPY
- ☐ FROTHY
- ☐ OTHER

SEDIMENT
- ☐ NONE
- ☐ SOME
- ☐ TONS

AROMA
- ☐ MALTY
- ☐ ROASTY
- ☐ HOPPY
- ☐ EARTHY
- ☐ FRUITY
- ☐ SOUR
- ☐ SPICY
- ☐ SMOKEY

NOTES

TASTE
- ☐ TART
- ☐ BITTER
- ☐ SWEET
- ☐ BOOZY

NOTES

PALATE (THE WAY THE BEER FEELS IN YOUR MOUTH)
- ☐ LIGHT-BODIED (THIN + WATERY)
- ☐ MEDIUM-BODIED (LIGHT + FULL)
- ☐ FULL-BODIED (RICH + CREAMY)
- ☐ EFFERVESCENT

NOTES

BEER TASTING NOTES

COMPARISONS

FOOD/MEAL PAIRINGS

SHARED WITH (FAMILY/FRIENDS)

RECOMMEND?
☐ YES ☐ NO

RATING
☐ 1 ☐ 2 ☐ 3 ☐ 4 ☐ 5 ☐ 6 ☐ 7 ☐ 8 ☐ 9 ☐ 10

SUMMARY

BEER TASTING NOTES

BEER NAME

BREWERY

TASTING DATE: **STYLE**

ALCOHOL BY VOLUME: **BOTTLED BY / BEST BY**   **PRICE**

CONTAINER
- ☐ BOTTLE
- ☐ CAN
- ☐ DRAFT
- ☐ GROWLER
- ☐ CASK
- ☐ OTHER

APPEARANCE
- ☐ GOLDEN
- ☐ AMBER
- ☐ COPPER
- ☐ RED
- ☐ BROWN
- ☐ BLACK
- ☐ OTHER

CLARITY
- ☐ CRYSTAL
- ☐ CLEAR
- ☐ HAZY
- ☐ OPAQUE
- ☐ OTHER

HEAD SIZE

HEAD RETENTION

HEAD DESCRIPTION
- ☐ SPARSE
- ☐ LIGHT
- ☐ CREAMY
- ☐ SOAPY
- ☐ FROTHY
- ☐ OTHER

SEDIMENT
- ☐ NONE
- ☐ SOME
- ☐ TONS

AROMA
- ☐ MALTY
- ☐ ROASTY
- ☐ HOPPY
- ☐ EARTHY
- ☐ FRUITY
- ☐ SOUR
- ☐ SPICY
- ☐ SMOKEY

NOTES

TASTE
- ☐ TART
- ☐ BITTER
- ☐ SWEET
- ☐ BOOZY

NOTES

PALATE (THE WAY THE BEER FEELS IN YOUR MOUTH)
- ☐ LIGHT-BODIED (THIN + WATERY)
- ☐ MEDIUM-BODIED (LIGHT + FULL)
- ☐ FULL-BODIED (RICH + CREAMY)
- ☐ EFFERVESCENT

NOTES

BEER TASTING NOTES

COMPARISONS

FOOD/MEAL PAIRINGS

SHARED WITH (FAMILY/FRIENDS)

RECOMMEND? ☐ YES ☐ NO

RATING ☐ 1 ☐ 2 ☐ 3 ☐ 4 ☐ 5 ☐ 6 ☐ 7 ☐ 8 ☐ 9 ☐ 10

SUMMARY

BEER TASTING NOTES

BEER NAME

BREWERY

TASTING DATE: STYLE

ALCOHOL BY VOLUME: BOTTLED BY / BEST BY   PRICE

CONTAINER	APPEARANCE	CLARITY	HEAD SIZE	
☐ BOTTLE	☐ GOLDEN	☐ CRYSTAL	HEAD RETENTION	
☐ CAN	☐ AMBER	☐ CLEAR		
☐ DRAFT	☐ COPPER	☐ HAZY	HEAD DESCRIPTION	SEDIMENT
☐ GROWLER	☐ RED	☐ OPAQUE	☐ SPARSE ☐ OTHER	☐ NONE
☐ CASK	☐ BROWN	☐ OTHER	☐ LIGHT	☐ SOME
☐ OTHER	☐ BLACK		☐ CREAMY	☐ TONS
	☐ OTHER		☐ SOAPY	
			☐ FROTHY	

AROMA

☐ MALTY
☐ ROASTY
☐ HOPPY
☐ EARTHY
☐ FRUITY
☐ SOUR
☐ SPICY
☐ SMOKEY

NOTES
....
....
....
....
....

TASTE

☐ TART
☐ BITTER
☐ SWEET
☐ BOOZY

NOTES
....
....

PALATE (THE WAY THE BEER FEELS IN YOUR MOUTH)

☐ LIGHT-BODIED (THIN + WATERY)
☐ MEDIUM-BODIED (LIGHT + FULL)
☐ FULL-BODIED (RICH + CREAMY)
☐ EFFERVESCENT

NOTES
....
....

BEER TASTING NOTES

COMPARISONS

FOOD/MEAL PAIRINGS

SHARED WITH (FAMILY/FRIENDS)

RECOMMEND?　　☐ YES　☐ NO

RATING　☐ 1　☐ 2　☐ 3　☐ 4　☐ 5　☐ 6　☐ 7　☐ 8　☐ 9　☐ 10

SUMMARY

BEER TASTING NOTES

BEER NAME

BREWERY

TASTING DATE:　　　　　　　　　　**STYLE**

ALCOHOL BY VOLUME:　　　**BOTTLED BY / BEST BY**　　　**PRICE**

CONTAINER
- ☐ BOTTLE
- ☐ CAN
- ☐ DRAFT
- ☐ GROWLER
- ☐ CASK
- ☐ OTHER

APPEARANCE
- ☐ GOLDEN
- ☐ AMBER
- ☐ COPPER
- ☐ RED
- ☐ BROWN
- ☐ BLACK
- ☐ OTHER

CLARITY
- ☐ CRYSTAL
- ☐ CLEAR
- ☐ HAZY
- ☐ OPAQUE
- ☐ OTHER

HEAD SIZE

HEAD RETENTION

HEAD DESCRIPTION
- ☐ SPARSE
- ☐ LIGHT
- ☐ CREAMY
- ☐ SOAPY
- ☐ FROTHY
- ☐ OTHER

SEDIMENT
- ☐ NONE
- ☐ SOME
- ☐ TONS

AROMA
- ☐ MALTY
- ☐ ROASTY
- ☐ HOPPY
- ☐ EARTHY
- ☐ FRUITY
- ☐ SOUR
- ☐ SPICY
- ☐ SMOKEY

NOTES

TASTE
- ☐ TART
- ☐ BITTER
- ☐ SWEET
- ☐ BOOZY

NOTES

PALATE (THE WAY THE BEER FEELS IN YOUR MOUTH)
- ☐ LIGHT-BODIED (THIN + WATERY)
- ☐ MEDIUM-BODIED (LIGHT + FULL)
- ☐ FULL-BODIED (RICH + CREAMY)
- ☐ EFFERVESCENT

NOTES

BEER TASTING NOTES

COMPARISONS

FOOD/MEAL PAIRINGS

SHARED WITH (FAMILY/FRIENDS)

RECOMMEND?
☐ YES   ☐ NO

RATING
☐ 1 ☐ 2 ☐ 3 ☐ 4 ☐ 5 ☐ 6 ☐ 7 ☐ 8 ☐ 9 ☐ 10

SUMMARY

BEER TASTING NOTES

BEER NAME

BREWERY

TASTING DATE: **STYLE**

ALCOHOL BY VOLUME: **BOTTLED BY / BEST BY** **PRICE**

CONTAINER
- ☐ BOTTLE
- ☐ CAN
- ☐ DRAFT
- ☐ GROWLER
- ☐ CASK
- ☐ OTHER

APPEARANCE
- ☐ GOLDEN
- ☐ AMBER
- ☐ COPPER
- ☐ RED
- ☐ BROWN
- ☐ BLACK
- ☐ OTHER

CLARITY
- ☐ CRYSTAL
- ☐ CLEAR
- ☐ HAZY
- ☐ OPAQUE
- ☐ OTHER

HEAD SIZE

HEAD RETENTION

HEAD DESCRIPTION
- ☐ SPARSE
- ☐ LIGHT
- ☐ CREAMY
- ☐ SOAPY
- ☐ FROTHY
- ☐ OTHER

SEDIMENT
- ☐ NONE
- ☐ SOME
- ☐ TONS

AROMA
- ☐ MALTY
- ☐ ROASTY
- ☐ HOPPY
- ☐ EARTHY
- ☐ FRUITY
- ☐ SOUR
- ☐ SPICY
- ☐ SMOKEY

NOTES

TASTE
- ☐ TART
- ☐ BITTER
- ☐ SWEET
- ☐ BOOZY

NOTES

PALATE (THE WAY THE BEER FEELS IN YOUR MOUTH)
- ☐ LIGHT-BODIED (THIN + WATERY)
- ☐ MEDIUM-BODIED (LIGHT + FULL)
- ☐ FULL-BODIED (RICH + CREAMY)
- ☐ EFFERVESCENT

NOTES

BEER TASTING NOTES

COMPARISONS

FOOD/MEAL PAIRINGS

SHARED WITH (FAMILY/FRIENDS)

RECOMMEND?　　　RATING

☐ YES　☐ NO　　☐ 1　☐ 2　☐ 3　☐ 4　☐ 5　☐ 6　☐ 7　☐ 8　☐ 9　☐ 10

SUMMARY

BEER TASTING NOTES

BEER NAME

BREWERY

TASTING DATE: **STYLE**

ALCOHOL BY VOLUME: **BOTTLED BY / BEST BY** **PRICE**

CONTAINER
- ☐ BOTTLE
- ☐ CAN
- ☐ DRAFT
- ☐ GROWLER
- ☐ CASK
- ☐ OTHER

APPEARANCE
- ☐ GOLDEN
- ☐ AMBER
- ☐ COPPER
- ☐ RED
- ☐ BROWN
- ☐ BLACK
- ☐ OTHER

CLARITY
- ☐ CRYSTAL
- ☐ CLEAR
- ☐ HAZY
- ☐ OPAQUE
- ☐ OTHER

HEAD SIZE

HEAD RETENTION

HEAD DESCRIPTION
- ☐ SPARSE   ☐ OTHER
- ☐ LIGHT
- ☐ CREAMY
- ☐ SOAPY
- ☐ FROTHY

SEDIMENT
- ☐ NONE
- ☐ SOME
- ☐ TONS

AROMA
- ☐ MALTY
- ☐ ROASTY
- ☐ HOPPY
- ☐ EARTHY
- ☐ FRUITY
- ☐ SOUR
- ☐ SPICY
- ☐ SMOKEY

NOTES

TASTE
- ☐ TART
- ☐ BITTER
- ☐ SWEET
- ☐ BOOZY

NOTES

PALATE (THE WAY THE BEER FEELS IN YOUR MOUTH)
- ☐ LIGHT-BODIED (THIN + WATERY)
- ☐ MEDIUM-BODIED (LIGHT + FULL)
- ☐ FULL-BODIED (RICH + CREAMY)
- ☐ EFFERVESCENT

NOTES

BEER TASTING NOTES

COMPARISONS

FOOD/MEAL PAIRINGS

SHARED WITH (FAMILY/FRIENDS)

RECOMMEND?
☐ YES   ☐ NO

RATING
☐ 1   ☐ 2   ☐ 3   ☐ 4   ☐ 5   ☐ 6   ☐ 7   ☐ 8   ☐ 9   ☐ 10

SUMMARY

BEER TASTING NOTES

BEER NAME

BREWERY

TASTING DATE: STYLE

ALCOHOL BY VOLUME: BOTTLED BY / BEST BY   PRICE

CONTAINER
- [ ] BOTTLE
- [ ] CAN
- [ ] DRAFT
- [ ] GROWLER
- [ ] CASK
- [ ] OTHER

APPEARANCE
- [ ] GOLDEN
- [ ] AMBER
- [ ] COPPER
- [ ] RED
- [ ] BROWN
- [ ] BLACK
- [ ] OTHER

CLARITY
- [ ] CRYSTAL
- [ ] CLEAR
- [ ] HAZY
- [ ] OPAQUE
- [ ] OTHER

HEAD SIZE

HEAD RETENTION

HEAD DESCRIPTION
- [ ] SPARSE
- [ ] LIGHT
- [ ] CREAMY
- [ ] SOAPY
- [ ] FROTHY
- [ ] OTHER

SEDIMENT
- [ ] NONE
- [ ] SOME
- [ ] TONS

AROMA
- [ ] MALTY
- [ ] ROASTY
- [ ] HOPPY
- [ ] EARTHY
- [ ] FRUITY
- [ ] SOUR
- [ ] SPICY
- [ ] SMOKEY

NOTES

TASTE
- [ ] TART
- [ ] BITTER
- [ ] SWEET
- [ ] BOOZY

NOTES

PALATE (THE WAY THE BEER FEELS IN YOUR MOUTH)
- [ ] LIGHT-BODIED (THIN + WATERY)
- [ ] MEDIUM-BODIED (LIGHT + FULL)
- [ ] FULL-BODIED (RICH + CREAMY)
- [ ] EFFERVESCENT

NOTES

BEER TASTING NOTES

COMPARISONS

FOOD/MEAL PAIRINGS

SHARED WITH (FAMILY/FRIENDS)

RECOMMEND?
☐ YES   ☐ NO

RATING
☐ 1 ☐ 2 ☐ 3 ☐ 4 ☐ 5 ☐ 6 ☐ 7 ☐ 8 ☐ 9 ☐ 10

SUMMARY

BEER TASTING NOTES

BEER NAME

BREWERY

TASTING DATE: **STYLE**

ALCOHOL BY VOLUME: **BOTTLED BY / BEST BY**   **PRICE**

CONTAINER	APPEARANCE	CLARITY	HEAD SIZE	
☐ BOTTLE	☐ GOLDEN	☐ CRYSTAL	**HEAD RETENTION**	
☐ CAN	☐ AMBER	☐ CLEAR		
☐ DRAFT	☐ COPPER	☐ HAZY	**HEAD DESCRIPTION**	**SEDIMENT**
☐ GROWLER	☐ RED	☐ OPAQUE	☐ SPARSE ☐ OTHER	☐ NONE
☐ CASK	☐ BROWN	☐ OTHER	☐ LIGHT	☐ SOME
☐ OTHER	☐ BLACK		☐ CREAMY	☐ TONS
	☐ OTHER		☐ SOAPY	
			☐ FROTHY	

AROMA

☐ MALTY   **NOTES**
☐ ROASTY
☐ HOPPY
☐ EARTHY
☐ FRUITY
☐ SOUR
☐ SPICY
☐ SMOKEY

TASTE

☐ TART   **NOTES**
☐ BITTER
☐ SWEET
☐ BOOZY

PALATE (THE WAY THE BEER FEELS IN YOUR MOUTH)

☐ LIGHT-BODIED (THIN + WATERY)   **NOTES**
☐ MEDIUM-BODIED (LIGHT + FULL)
☐ FULL-BODIED (RICH + CREAMY)
☐ EFFERVESCENT

BEER TASTING NOTES

COMPARISONS

FOOD/MEAL PAIRINGS

SHARED WITH (FAMILY/FRIENDS)

RECOMMEND? ☐ YES ☐ NO

RATING ☐ 1 ☐ 2 ☐ 3 ☐ 4 ☐ 5 ☐ 6 ☐ 7 ☐ 8 ☐ 9 ☐ 10

SUMMARY

BEER TASTING NOTES

BEER NAME

BREWERY

TASTING DATE: STYLE

ALCOHOL BY VOLUME: BOTTLED BY / BEST BY PRICE

CONTAINER
- [ ] BOTTLE
- [ ] CAN
- [ ] DRAFT
- [ ] GROWLER
- [ ] CASK
- [ ] OTHER

APPEARANCE
- [ ] GOLDEN
- [ ] AMBER
- [ ] COPPER
- [ ] RED
- [ ] BROWN
- [ ] BLACK
- [ ] OTHER

CLARITY
- [ ] CRYSTAL
- [ ] CLEAR
- [ ] HAZY
- [ ] OPAQUE
- [ ] OTHER

HEAD SIZE

HEAD RETENTION

HEAD DESCRIPTION
- [ ] SPARSE
- [ ] LIGHT
- [ ] CREAMY
- [ ] SOAPY
- [ ] FROTHY
- [ ] OTHER

SEDIMENT
- [ ] NONE
- [ ] SOME
- [ ] TONS

AROMA
- [ ] MALTY
- [ ] ROASTY
- [ ] HOPPY
- [ ] EARTHY
- [ ] FRUITY
- [ ] SOUR
- [ ] SPICY
- [ ] SMOKEY

NOTES

TASTE
- [ ] TART
- [ ] BITTER
- [ ] SWEET
- [ ] BOOZY

NOTES

PALATE (THE WAY THE BEER FEELS IN YOUR MOUTH)
- [ ] LIGHT-BODIED (THIN + WATERY)
- [ ] MEDIUM-BODIED (LIGHT + FULL)
- [ ] FULL-BODIED (RICH + CREAMY)
- [ ] EFFERVESCENT

NOTES

BEER TASTING NOTES

COMPARISONS

FOOD/MEAL PAIRINGS

SHARED WITH (FAMILY/FRIENDS)

RECOMMEND? ☐ YES ☐ NO

RATING ☐ 1 ☐ 2 ☐ 3 ☐ 4 ☐ 5 ☐ 6 ☐ 7 ☐ 8 ☐ 9 ☐ 10

SUMMARY

BEER TASTING NOTES

BEER NAME

BREWERY

TASTING DATE: STYLE

ALCOHOL BY VOLUME: BOTTLED BY / BEST BY PRICE

CONTAINER	APPEARANCE	CLARITY	HEAD SIZE	
☐ BOTTLE	☐ GOLDEN	☐ CRYSTAL	HEAD RETENTION	
☐ CAN	☐ AMBER	☐ CLEAR		
☐ DRAFT	☐ COPPER	☐ HAZY	HEAD DESCRIPTION	SEDIMENT
☐ GROWLER	☐ RED	☐ OPAQUE	☐ SPARSE ☐ OTHER	☐ NONE
☐ CASK	☐ BROWN	☐ OTHER	☐ LIGHT	☐ SOME
☐ OTHER	☐ BLACK		☐ CREAMY	☐ TONS
	☐ OTHER		☐ SOAPY	
			☐ FROTHY	

AROMA

☐ MALTY
☐ ROASTY
☐ HOPPY
☐ EARTHY
☐ FRUITY
☐ SOUR
☐ SPICY
☐ SMOKEY

NOTES

TASTE

☐ TART
☐ BITTER
☐ SWEET
☐ BOOZY

NOTES

PALATE (THE WAY THE BEER FEELS IN YOUR MOUTH)

☐ LIGHT-BODIED (THIN + WATERY)
☐ MEDIUM-BODIED (LIGHT + FULL)
☐ FULL-BODIED (RICH + CREAMY)
☐ EFFERVESCENT

NOTES

BEER TASTING NOTES

COMPARISONS

FOOD/MEAL PAIRINGS

SHARED WITH (FAMILY/FRIENDS)

RECOMMEND? ☐ YES ☐ NO

RATING ☐ 1 ☐ 2 ☐ 3 ☐ 4 ☐ 5 ☐ 6 ☐ 7 ☐ 8 ☐ 9 ☐ 10

SUMMARY

BEER TASTING NOTES

BEER NAME

BREWERY

TASTING DATE: **STYLE**

ALCOHOL BY VOLUME: **BOTTLED BY / BEST BY** **PRICE**

CONTAINER
- ☐ BOTTLE
- ☐ CAN
- ☐ DRAFT
- ☐ GROWLER
- ☐ CASK
- ☐ OTHER

APPEARANCE
- ☐ GOLDEN
- ☐ AMBER
- ☐ COPPER
- ☐ RED
- ☐ BROWN
- ☐ BLACK
- ☐ OTHER

CLARITY
- ☐ CRYSTAL
- ☐ CLEAR
- ☐ HAZY
- ☐ OPAQUE
- ☐ OTHER

HEAD SIZE

HEAD RETENTION

HEAD DESCRIPTION
- ☐ SPARSE
- ☐ OTHER
- ☐ LIGHT
- ☐ CREAMY
- ☐ SOAPY
- ☐ FROTHY

SEDIMENT
- ☐ NONE
- ☐ SOME
- ☐ TONS

AROMA
- ☐ MALTY
- ☐ ROASTY
- ☐ HOPPY
- ☐ EARTHY
- ☐ FRUITY
- ☐ SOUR
- ☐ SPICY
- ☐ SMOKEY

NOTES

TASTE
- ☐ TART
- ☐ BITTER
- ☐ SWEET
- ☐ BOOZY

NOTES

PALATE (THE WAY THE BEER FEELS IN YOUR MOUTH)
- ☐ LIGHT-BODIED (THIN + WATERY)
- ☐ MEDIUM-BODIED (LIGHT + FULL)
- ☐ FULL-BODIED (RICH + CREAMY)
- ☐ EFFERVESCENT

NOTES

BEER TASTING NOTES

COMPARISONS

FOOD/MEAL PAIRINGS

SHARED WITH (FAMILY/FRIENDS)

RECOMMEND? ☐ YES ☐ NO

RATING ☐ 1 ☐ 2 ☐ 3 ☐ 4 ☐ 5 ☐ 6 ☐ 7 ☐ 8 ☐ 9 ☐ 10

SUMMARY

BEER TASTING NOTES

BEER NAME

BREWERY

TASTING DATE: **STYLE**

ALCOHOL BY VOLUME: **BOTTLED BY / BEST BY** **PRICE**

CONTAINER

- ☐ BOTTLE
- ☐ CAN
- ☐ DRAFT
- ☐ GROWLER
- ☐ CASK
- ☐ OTHER

APPEARANCE

- ☐ GOLDEN
- ☐ AMBER
- ☐ COPPER
- ☐ RED
- ☐ BROWN
- ☐ BLACK
- ☐ OTHER

CLARITY

- ☐ CRYSTAL
- ☐ CLEAR
- ☐ HAZY
- ☐ OPAQUE
- ☐ OTHER

HEAD SIZE

HEAD RETENTION

HEAD DESCRIPTION

- ☐ SPARSE
- ☐ OTHER
- ☐ LIGHT
- ☐ CREAMY
- ☐ SOAPY
- ☐ FROTHY

SEDIMENT

- ☐ NONE
- ☐ SOME
- ☐ TONS

AROMA

- ☐ MALTY
- ☐ ROASTY
- ☐ HOPPY
- ☐ EARTHY
- ☐ FRUITY
- ☐ SOUR
- ☐ SPICY
- ☐ SMOKEY

NOTES

TASTE

- ☐ TART
- ☐ BITTER
- ☐ SWEET
- ☐ BOOZY

NOTES

PALATE (THE WAY THE BEER FEELS IN YOUR MOUTH)

- ☐ LIGHT-BODIED (THIN + WATERY)
- ☐ MEDIUM-BODIED (LIGHT + FULL)
- ☐ FULL-BODIED (RICH + CREAMY)
- ☐ EFFERVESCENT

NOTES

BEER TASTING NOTES

COMPARISONS

FOOD/MEAL PAIRINGS

SHARED WITH (FAMILY/FRIENDS)

RECOMMEND? ☐ YES ☐ NO

RATING ☐ 1 ☐ 2 ☐ 3 ☐ 4 ☐ 5 ☐ 6 ☐ 7 ☐ 8 ☐ 9 ☐ 10

SUMMARY

BEER TASTING NOTES

BEER NAME

BREWERY

TASTING DATE: **STYLE**

ALCOHOL BY VOLUME: **BOTTLED BY / BEST BY**   **PRICE**

CONTAINER
- [ ] BOTTLE
- [ ] CAN
- [ ] DRAFT
- [ ] GROWLER
- [ ] CASK
- [ ] OTHER

APPEARANCE
- [ ] GOLDEN
- [ ] AMBER
- [ ] COPPER
- [ ] RED
- [ ] BROWN
- [ ] BLACK
- [ ] OTHER

CLARITY
- [ ] CRYSTAL
- [ ] CLEAR
- [ ] HAZY
- [ ] OPAQUE
- [ ] OTHER

HEAD SIZE

HEAD RETENTION

HEAD DESCRIPTION
- [ ] SPARSE
- [ ] LIGHT
- [ ] CREAMY
- [ ] SOAPY
- [ ] FROTHY
- [ ] OTHER

SEDIMENT
- [ ] NONE
- [ ] SOME
- [ ] TONS

AROMA
- [ ] MALTY
- [ ] ROASTY
- [ ] HOPPY
- [ ] EARTHY
- [ ] FRUITY
- [ ] SOUR
- [ ] SPICY
- [ ] SMOKEY

NOTES

TASTE
- [ ] TART
- [ ] BITTER
- [ ] SWEET
- [ ] BOOZY

NOTES

PALATE (THE WAY THE BEER FEELS IN YOUR MOUTH)
- [ ] LIGHT-BODIED (THIN + WATERY)
- [ ] MEDIUM-BODIED (LIGHT + FULL)
- [ ] FULL-BODIED (RICH + CREAMY)
- [ ] EFFERVESCENT

NOTES

BEER TASTING NOTES

COMPARISONS

FOOD/MEAL PAIRINGS

SHARED WITH (FAMILY/FRIENDS)

RECOMMEND?
- [ ] YES
- [ ] NO

RATING
- [ ] 1
- [ ] 2
- [ ] 3
- [ ] 4
- [ ] 5
- [ ] 6
- [ ] 7
- [ ] 8
- [ ] 9
- [ ] 10

SUMMARY

BEER TASTING NOTES

BEER NAME

BREWERY

TASTING DATE: **STYLE**

ALCOHOL BY VOLUME: **BOTTLED BY / BEST BY** **PRICE**

CONTAINER	APPEARANCE	CLARITY	HEAD SIZE	
☐ BOTTLE	☐ GOLDEN	☐ CRYSTAL	**HEAD RETENTION**	
☐ CAN	☐ AMBER	☐ CLEAR		
☐ DRAFT	☐ COPPER	☐ HAZY	**HEAD DESCRIPTION**	**SEDIMENT**
☐ GROWLER	☐ RED	☐ OPAQUE	☐ SPARSE ☐ OTHER	☐ NONE
☐ CASK	☐ BROWN	☐ OTHER	☐ LIGHT	☐ SOME
☐ OTHER	☐ BLACK		☐ CREAMY	☐ TONS
	☐ OTHER		☐ SOAPY	
			☐ FROTHY	

AROMA

☐ MALTY **NOTES**
☐ ROASTY
☐ HOPPY
☐ EARTHY
☐ FRUITY
☐ SOUR
☐ SPICY
☐ SMOKEY

TASTE

☐ TART **NOTES**
☐ BITTER
☐ SWEET
☐ BOOZY

PALATE (THE WAY THE BEER FEELS IN YOUR MOUTH)

☐ LIGHT-BODIED (THIN + WATERY) **NOTES**
☐ MEDIUM-BODIED (LIGHT + FULL)
☐ FULL-BODIED (RICH + CREAMY)
☐ EFFERVESCENT

BEER TASTING NOTES

COMPARISONS

FOOD/MEAL PAIRINGS

SHARED WITH (FAMILY/FRIENDS)

RECOMMEND? ☐ YES ☐ NO

RATING ☐ 1 ☐ 2 ☐ 3 ☐ 4 ☐ 5 ☐ 6 ☐ 7 ☐ 8 ☐ 9 ☐ 10

SUMMARY

BEER TASTING NOTES

BEER NAME

BREWERY

TASTING DATE: **STYLE**

ALCOHOL BY VOLUME: **BOTTLED BY / BEST BY**   **PRICE**

CONTAINER
- ☐ BOTTLE
- ☐ CAN
- ☐ DRAFT
- ☐ GROWLER
- ☐ CASK
- ☐ OTHER

APPEARANCE
- ☐ GOLDEN
- ☐ AMBER
- ☐ COPPER
- ☐ RED
- ☐ BROWN
- ☐ BLACK
- ☐ OTHER

CLARITY
- ☐ CRYSTAL
- ☐ CLEAR
- ☐ HAZY
- ☐ OPAQUE
- ☐ OTHER

HEAD SIZE

HEAD RETENTION

HEAD DESCRIPTION
- ☐ SPARSE
- ☐ OTHER
- ☐ LIGHT
- ☐ CREAMY
- ☐ SOAPY
- ☐ FROTHY

SEDIMENT
- ☐ NONE
- ☐ SOME
- ☐ TONS

AROMA
- ☐ MALTY
- ☐ ROASTY
- ☐ HOPPY
- ☐ EARTHY
- ☐ FRUITY
- ☐ SOUR
- ☐ SPICY
- ☐ SMOKEY

NOTES

TASTE
- ☐ TART
- ☐ BITTER
- ☐ SWEET
- ☐ BOOZY

NOTES

PALATE (THE WAY THE BEER FEELS IN YOUR MOUTH)
- ☐ LIGHT-BODIED (THIN + WATERY)
- ☐ MEDIUM-BODIED (LIGHT + FULL)
- ☐ FULL-BODIED (RICH + CREAMY)
- ☐ EFFERVESCENT

NOTES

BEER TASTING NOTES

COMPARISONS

FOOD/MEAL PAIRINGS

SHARED WITH (FAMILY/FRIENDS)

RECOMMEND? RATING
☐ YES ☐ NO   ☐ 1 ☐ 2 ☐ 3 ☐ 4 ☐ 5 ☐ 6 ☐ 7 ☐ 8 ☐ 9 ☐ 10

SUMMARY

BEER TASTING NOTES

BEER NAME

BREWERY

TASTING DATE: STYLE

ALCOHOL BY VOLUME: BOTTLED BY / BEST BY   PRICE

CONTAINER
- [ ] BOTTLE
- [ ] CAN
- [ ] DRAFT
- [ ] GROWLER
- [ ] CASK
- [ ] OTHER

APPEARANCE
- [ ] GOLDEN
- [ ] AMBER
- [ ] COPPER
- [ ] RED
- [ ] BROWN
- [ ] BLACK
- [ ] OTHER

CLARITY
- [ ] CRYSTAL
- [ ] CLEAR
- [ ] HAZY
- [ ] OPAQUE
- [ ] OTHER

HEAD SIZE

HEAD RETENTION

HEAD DESCRIPTION
- [ ] SPARSE
- [ ] LIGHT
- [ ] CREAMY
- [ ] SOAPY
- [ ] FROTHY
- [ ] OTHER

SEDIMENT
- [ ] NONE
- [ ] SOME
- [ ] TONS

AROMA
- [ ] MALTY
- [ ] ROASTY
- [ ] HOPPY
- [ ] EARTHY
- [ ] FRUITY
- [ ] SOUR
- [ ] SPICY
- [ ] SMOKEY

NOTES

TASTE
- [ ] TART
- [ ] BITTER
- [ ] SWEET
- [ ] BOOZY

NOTES

PALATE (THE WAY THE BEER FEELS IN YOUR MOUTH)
- [ ] LIGHT-BODIED (THIN + WATERY)
- [ ] MEDIUM-BODIED (LIGHT + FULL)
- [ ] FULL-BODIED (RICH + CREAMY)
- [ ] EFFERVESCENT

NOTES

BEER TASTING NOTES

COMPARISONS

FOOD/MEAL PAIRINGS

SHARED WITH (FAMILY/FRIENDS)

RECOMMEND? ☐ YES ☐ NO

RATING ☐ 1 ☐ 2 ☐ 3 ☐ 4 ☐ 5 ☐ 6 ☐ 7 ☐ 8 ☐ 9 ☐ 10

SUMMARY

BEER TASTING NOTES

BEER NAME

BREWERY

TASTING DATE: **STYLE**

ALCOHOL BY VOLUME: **BOTTLED BY / BEST BY** **PRICE**

CONTAINER
- ☐ BOTTLE
- ☐ CAN
- ☐ DRAFT
- ☐ GROWLER
- ☐ CASK
- ☐ OTHER

APPEARANCE
- ☐ GOLDEN
- ☐ AMBER
- ☐ COPPER
- ☐ RED
- ☐ BROWN
- ☐ BLACK
- ☐ OTHER

CLARITY
- ☐ CRYSTAL
- ☐ CLEAR
- ☐ HAZY
- ☐ OPAQUE
- ☐ OTHER

HEAD SIZE

HEAD RETENTION

HEAD DESCRIPTION
- ☐ SPARSE   ☐ OTHER
- ☐ LIGHT
- ☐ CREAMY
- ☐ SOAPY
- ☐ FROTHY

SEDIMENT
- ☐ NONE
- ☐ SOME
- ☐ TONS

AROMA
- ☐ MALTY
- ☐ ROASTY
- ☐ HOPPY
- ☐ EARTHY
- ☐ FRUITY
- ☐ SOUR
- ☐ SPICY
- ☐ SMOKEY

NOTES

TASTE
- ☐ TART
- ☐ BITTER
- ☐ SWEET
- ☐ BOOZY

NOTES

PALATE (THE WAY THE BEER FEELS IN YOUR MOUTH)
- ☐ LIGHT-BODIED (THIN + WATERY)
- ☐ MEDIUM-BODIED (LIGHT + FULL)
- ☐ FULL-BODIED (RICH + CREAMY)
- ☐ EFFERVESCENT

NOTES

BEER TASTING NOTES

COMPARISONS

FOOD/MEAL PAIRINGS

SHARED WITH (FAMILY/FRIENDS)

RECOMMEND?
☐ YES ☐ NO

RATING
☐ 1 ☐ 2 ☐ 3 ☐ 4 ☐ 5 ☐ 6 ☐ 7 ☐ 8 ☐ 9 ☐ 10

SUMMARY

BEER TASTING NOTES

BEER NAME

BREWERY

TASTING DATE: STYLE

ALCOHOL BY VOLUME: BOTTLED BY / BEST BY   PRICE

CONTAINER
- ☐ BOTTLE
- ☐ CAN
- ☐ DRAFT
- ☐ GROWLER
- ☐ CASK
- ☐ OTHER

APPEARANCE
- ☐ GOLDEN
- ☐ AMBER
- ☐ COPPER
- ☐ RED
- ☐ BROWN
- ☐ BLACK
- ☐ OTHER

CLARITY
- ☐ CRYSTAL
- ☐ CLEAR
- ☐ HAZY
- ☐ OPAQUE
- ☐ OTHER

HEAD SIZE

HEAD RETENTION

HEAD DESCRIPTION
- ☐ SPARSE
- ☐ LIGHT
- ☐ CREAMY
- ☐ SOAPY
- ☐ FROTHY
- ☐ OTHER

SEDIMENT
- ☐ NONE
- ☐ SOME
- ☐ TONS

AROMA
- ☐ MALTY
- ☐ ROASTY
- ☐ HOPPY
- ☐ EARTHY
- ☐ FRUITY
- ☐ SOUR
- ☐ SPICY
- ☐ SMOKEY

NOTES

TASTE
- ☐ TART
- ☐ BITTER
- ☐ SWEET
- ☐ BOOZY

NOTES

PALATE (THE WAY THE BEER FEELS IN YOUR MOUTH)
- ☐ LIGHT-BODIED (THIN + WATERY)
- ☐ MEDIUM-BODIED (LIGHT + FULL)
- ☐ FULL-BODIED (RICH + CREAMY)
- ☐ EFFERVESCENT

NOTES

BEER TASTING NOTES

COMPARISONS

FOOD/MEAL PAIRINGS

SHARED WITH (FAMILY/FRIENDS)

RECOMMEND?
☐ YES ☐ NO

RATING
☐ 1 ☐ 2 ☐ 3 ☐ 4 ☐ 5 ☐ 6 ☐ 7 ☐ 8 ☐ 9 ☐ 10

SUMMARY

BEER TASTING NOTES

BEER NAME

BREWERY

TASTING DATE: **STYLE**

ALCOHOL BY VOLUME: **BOTTLED BY / BEST BY** **PRICE**

CONTAINER
- ☐ BOTTLE
- ☐ CAN
- ☐ DRAFT
- ☐ GROWLER
- ☐ CASK
- ☐ OTHER

APPEARANCE
- ☐ GOLDEN
- ☐ AMBER
- ☐ COPPER
- ☐ RED
- ☐ BROWN
- ☐ BLACK
- ☐ OTHER

CLARITY
- ☐ CRYSTAL
- ☐ CLEAR
- ☐ HAZY
- ☐ OPAQUE
- ☐ OTHER

HEAD SIZE

HEAD RETENTION

HEAD DESCRIPTION
- ☐ SPARSE
- ☐ OTHER
- ☐ LIGHT
- ☐ CREAMY
- ☐ SOAPY
- ☐ FROTHY

SEDIMENT
- ☐ NONE
- ☐ SOME
- ☐ TONS

AROMA
- ☐ MALTY
- ☐ ROASTY
- ☐ HOPPY
- ☐ EARTHY
- ☐ FRUITY
- ☐ SOUR
- ☐ SPICY
- ☐ SMOKEY

NOTES

TASTE
- ☐ TART
- ☐ BITTER
- ☐ SWEET
- ☐ BOOZY

NOTES

PALATE (THE WAY THE BEER FEELS IN YOUR MOUTH)
- ☐ LIGHT-BODIED (THIN + WATERY)
- ☐ MEDIUM-BODIED (LIGHT + FULL)
- ☐ FULL-BODIED (RICH + CREAMY)
- ☐ EFFERVESCENT

NOTES

BEER TASTING NOTES

COMPARISONS

FOOD/MEAL PAIRINGS

SHARED WITH (FAMILY/FRIENDS)

RECOMMEND?
☐ YES   ☐ NO

RATING
☐ 1   ☐ 2   ☐ 3   ☐ 4   ☐ 5   ☐ 6   ☐ 7   ☐ 8   ☐ 9   ☐ 10

SUMMARY

BEER TASTING NOTES

BEER NAME

BREWERY

TASTING DATE:　　　　　　　　　**STYLE**

ALCOHOL BY VOLUME:　　　**BOTTLED BY / BEST BY**　　　　**PRICE**

CONTAINER	**APPEARANCE**	**CLARITY**	**HEAD SIZE**	
			HEAD RETENTION	
☐ BOTTLE	☐ GOLDEN	☐ CRYSTAL		
☐ CAN	☐ AMBER	☐ CLEAR	**HEAD DESCRIPTION**	**SEDIMENT**
☐ DRAFT	☐ COPPER	☐ HAZY	☐ SPARSE ☐ OTHER	☐ NONE
☐ GROWLER	☐ RED	☐ OPAQUE	☐ LIGHT	☐ SOME
☐ CASK	☐ BROWN	☐ OTHER	☐ CREAMY	☐ TONS
☐ OTHER	☐ BLACK		☐ SOAPY	
	☐ OTHER		☐ FROTHY	

AROMA

☐ MALTY　　**NOTES**
☐ ROASTY
☐ HOPPY
☐ EARTHY
☐ FRUITY
☐ SOUR
☐ SPICY
☐ SMOKEY

TASTE

☐ TART　　**NOTES**
☐ BITTER
☐ SWEET
☐ BOOZY

PALATE (THE WAY THE BEER FEELS IN YOUR MOUTH)

☐ LIGHT-BODIED (THIN + WATERY)　　**NOTES**
☐ MEDIUM-BODIED (LIGHT + FULL)
☐ FULL-BODIED (RICH + CREAMY)
☐ EFFERVESCENT

BEER TASTING NOTES

COMPARISONS

FOOD/MEAL PAIRINGS

SHARED WITH (FAMILY/FRIENDS)

RECOMMEND?   ☐ YES   ☐ NO

RATING   ☐ 1   ☐ 2   ☐ 3   ☐ 4   ☐ 5   ☐ 6   ☐ 7   ☐ 8   ☐ 9   ☐ 10

SUMMARY

BEER TASTING NOTES

BEER NAME

BREWERY

TASTING DATE: **STYLE**

ALCOHOL BY VOLUME: **BOTTLED BY / BEST BY**   **PRICE**

CONTAINER	APPEARANCE	CLARITY	HEAD SIZE	
☐ BOTTLE	☐ GOLDEN	☐ CRYSTAL	**HEAD RETENTION**	
☐ CAN	☐ AMBER	☐ CLEAR		
☐ DRAFT	☐ COPPER	☐ HAZY	**HEAD DESCRIPTION**	**SEDIMENT**
☐ GROWLER	☐ RED	☐ OPAQUE	☐ SPARSE ☐ OTHER	☐ NONE
☐ CASK	☐ BROWN	☐ OTHER	☐ LIGHT	☐ SOME
☐ OTHER	☐ BLACK		☐ CREAMY	☐ TONS
	☐ OTHER		☐ SOAPY	
			☐ FROTHY	

AROMA

☐ MALTY   **NOTES**
☐ ROASTY
☐ HOPPY
☐ EARTHY
☐ FRUITY
☐ SOUR
☐ SPICY
☐ SMOKEY

TASTE

☐ TART   **NOTES**
☐ BITTER
☐ SWEET
☐ BOOZY

PALATE (THE WAY THE BEER FEELS IN YOUR MOUTH)

☐ LIGHT-BODIED (THIN + WATERY)   **NOTES**
☐ MEDIUM-BODIED (LIGHT + FULL)
☐ FULL-BODIED (RICH + CREAMY)
☐ EFFERVESCENT

BEER TASTING NOTES

COMPARISONS

FOOD/MEAL PAIRINGS

SHARED WITH (FAMILY/FRIENDS)

RECOMMEND? ☐ YES ☐ NO

RATING ☐ 1 ☐ 2 ☐ 3 ☐ 4 ☐ 5 ☐ 6 ☐ 7 ☐ 8 ☐ 9 ☐ 10

SUMMARY

BEER TASTING NOTES

BEER NAME

BREWERY

TASTING DATE: STYLE

ALCOHOL BY VOLUME: BOTTLED BY / BEST BY   PRICE

CONTAINER
- [ ] BOTTLE
- [ ] CAN
- [ ] DRAFT
- [ ] GROWLER
- [ ] CASK
- [ ] OTHER

APPEARANCE
- [ ] GOLDEN
- [ ] AMBER
- [ ] COPPER
- [ ] RED
- [ ] BROWN
- [ ] BLACK
- [ ] OTHER

CLARITY
- [ ] CRYSTAL
- [ ] CLEAR
- [ ] HAZY
- [ ] OPAQUE
- [ ] OTHER

HEAD SIZE

HEAD RETENTION

HEAD DESCRIPTION
- [ ] SPARSE
- [ ] LIGHT
- [ ] CREAMY
- [ ] SOAPY
- [ ] FROTHY
- [ ] OTHER

SEDIMENT
- [ ] NONE
- [ ] SOME
- [ ] TONS

AROMA
- [ ] MALTY
- [ ] ROASTY
- [ ] HOPPY
- [ ] EARTHY
- [ ] FRUITY
- [ ] SOUR
- [ ] SPICY
- [ ] SMOKEY

NOTES

TASTE
- [ ] TART
- [ ] BITTER
- [ ] SWEET
- [ ] BOOZY

NOTES

PALATE (THE WAY THE BEER FEELS IN YOUR MOUTH)
- [ ] LIGHT-BODIED (THIN + WATERY)
- [ ] MEDIUM-BODIED (LIGHT + FULL)
- [ ] FULL-BODIED (RICH + CREAMY)
- [ ] EFFERVESCENT

NOTES

BEER TASTING NOTES

COMPARISONS

FOOD/MEAL PAIRINGS

SHARED WITH (FAMILY/FRIENDS)

RECOMMEND?
☐ YES ☐ NO

RATING
☐ 1 ☐ 2 ☐ 3 ☐ 4 ☐ 5 ☐ 6 ☐ 7 ☐ 8 ☐ 9 ☐ 10

SUMMARY

BEER TASTING NOTES

BEER NAME

BREWERY

TASTING DATE: **STYLE**

ALCOHOL BY VOLUME: **BOTTLED BY / BEST BY** **PRICE**

CONTAINER	APPEARANCE	CLARITY	HEAD SIZE	
☐ BOTTLE	☐ GOLDEN	☐ CRYSTAL	**HEAD RETENTION**	
☐ CAN	☐ AMBER	☐ CLEAR		
☐ DRAFT	☐ COPPER	☐ HAZY	**HEAD DESCRIPTION**	**SEDIMENT**
☐ GROWLER	☐ RED	☐ OPAQUE	☐ SPARSE ☐ OTHER	☐ NONE
☐ CASK	☐ BROWN	☐ OTHER	☐ LIGHT	☐ SOME
☐ OTHER	☐ BLACK		☐ CREAMY	☐ TONS
	☐ OTHER		☐ SOAPY	
			☐ FROTHY	

AROMA

☐ MALTY
☐ ROASTY
☐ HOPPY
☐ EARTHY
☐ FRUITY
☐ SOUR
☐ SPICY
☐ SMOKEY

NOTES

TASTE

☐ TART
☐ BITTER
☐ SWEET
☐ BOOZY

NOTES

PALATE (THE WAY THE BEER FEELS IN YOUR MOUTH)

☐ LIGHT-BODIED (THIN + WATERY)
☐ MEDIUM-BODIED (LIGHT + FULL)
☐ FULL-BODIED (RICH + CREAMY)
☐ EFFERVESCENT

NOTES

BEER TASTING NOTES

COMPARISONS

FOOD/MEAL PAIRINGS

SHARED WITH (FAMILY/FRIENDS)

RECOMMEND?
☐ YES ☐ NO

RATING
☐ 1 ☐ 2 ☐ 3 ☐ 4 ☐ 5 ☐ 6 ☐ 7 ☐ 8 ☐ 9 ☐ 10

SUMMARY

BEER TASTING NOTES

BEER NAME

BREWERY

TASTING DATE: **STYLE**

ALCOHOL BY VOLUME: **BOTTLED BY / BEST BY**   **PRICE**

CONTAINER
- ☐ BOTTLE
- ☐ CAN
- ☐ DRAFT
- ☐ GROWLER
- ☐ CASK
- ☐ OTHER

APPEARANCE
- ☐ GOLDEN
- ☐ AMBER
- ☐ COPPER
- ☐ RED
- ☐ BROWN
- ☐ BLACK
- ☐ OTHER

CLARITY
- ☐ CRYSTAL
- ☐ CLEAR
- ☐ HAZY
- ☐ OPAQUE
- ☐ OTHER

HEAD SIZE

HEAD RETENTION

HEAD DESCRIPTION
- ☐ SPARSE
- ☐ LIGHT
- ☐ CREAMY
- ☐ SOAPY
- ☐ FROTHY
- ☐ OTHER

SEDIMENT
- ☐ NONE
- ☐ SOME
- ☐ TONS

AROMA
- ☐ MALTY
- ☐ ROASTY
- ☐ HOPPY
- ☐ EARTHY
- ☐ FRUITY
- ☐ SOUR
- ☐ SPICY
- ☐ SMOKEY

NOTES

TASTE
- ☐ TART
- ☐ BITTER
- ☐ SWEET
- ☐ BOOZY

NOTES

PALATE (THE WAY THE BEER FEELS IN YOUR MOUTH)
- ☐ LIGHT-BODIED (THIN + WATERY)
- ☐ MEDIUM-BODIED (LIGHT + FULL)
- ☐ FULL-BODIED (RICH + CREAMY)
- ☐ EFFERVESCENT

NOTES

BEER TASTING NOTES

COMPARISONS

FOOD/MEAL PAIRINGS

SHARED WITH (FAMILY/FRIENDS)

RECOMMEND?
☐ YES   ☐ NO

RATING
☐ 1 ☐ 2 ☐ 3 ☐ 4 ☐ 5 ☐ 6 ☐ 7 ☐ 8 ☐ 9 ☐ 10

SUMMARY

BEER TASTING NOTES

BEER NAME

BREWERY

TASTING DATE: **STYLE**

ALCOHOL BY VOLUME: **BOTTLED BY / BEST BY** **PRICE**

CONTAINER
- [ ] BOTTLE
- [ ] CAN
- [ ] DRAFT
- [ ] GROWLER
- [ ] CASK
- [ ] OTHER

APPEARANCE
- [ ] GOLDEN
- [ ] AMBER
- [ ] COPPER
- [ ] RED
- [ ] BROWN
- [ ] BLACK
- [ ] OTHER

CLARITY
- [ ] CRYSTAL
- [ ] CLEAR
- [ ] HAZY
- [ ] OPAQUE
- [ ] OTHER

HEAD SIZE

HEAD RETENTION

HEAD DESCRIPTION
- [ ] SPARSE
- [ ] OTHER
- [ ] LIGHT
- [ ] CREAMY
- [ ] SOAPY
- [ ] FROTHY

SEDIMENT
- [ ] NONE
- [ ] SOME
- [ ] TONS

AROMA
- [ ] MALTY
- [ ] ROASTY
- [ ] HOPPY
- [ ] EARTHY
- [ ] FRUITY
- [ ] SOUR
- [ ] SPICY
- [ ] SMOKEY

NOTES

TASTE
- [ ] TART
- [ ] BITTER
- [ ] SWEET
- [ ] BOOZY

NOTES

PALATE (THE WAY THE BEER FEELS IN YOUR MOUTH)
- [ ] LIGHT-BODIED (THIN + WATERY)
- [ ] MEDIUM-BODIED (LIGHT + FULL)
- [ ] FULL-BODIED (RICH + CREAMY)
- [ ] EFFERVESCENT

NOTES

BEER TASTING NOTES

COMPARISONS

FOOD/MEAL PAIRINGS

SHARED WITH (FAMILY/FRIENDS)

RECOMMEND?
☐ YES ☐ NO

RATING
☐ 1 ☐ 2 ☐ 3 ☐ 4 ☐ 5 ☐ 6 ☐ 7 ☐ 8 ☐ 9 ☐ 10

SUMMARY

BEER TASTING NOTES

BEER NAME

BREWERY

TASTING DATE: **STYLE**

ALCOHOL BY VOLUME: **BOTTLED BY / BEST BY** **PRICE**

CONTAINER	APPEARANCE	CLARITY	HEAD SIZE	
☐ BOTTLE	☐ GOLDEN	☐ CRYSTAL	**HEAD RETENTION**	
☐ CAN	☐ AMBER	☐ CLEAR		
☐ DRAFT	☐ COPPER	☐ HAZY	**HEAD DESCRIPTION**	**SEDIMENT**
☐ GROWLER	☐ RED	☐ OPAQUE	☐ SPARSE ☐ OTHER	☐ NONE
☐ CASK	☐ BROWN	☐ OTHER	☐ LIGHT	☐ SOME
☐ OTHER	☐ BLACK		☐ CREAMY	☐ TONS
	☐ OTHER		☐ SOAPY	
			☐ FROTHY	

AROMA

☐ MALTY
☐ ROASTY
☐ HOPPY
☐ EARTHY
☐ FRUITY
☐ SOUR
☐ SPICY
☐ SMOKEY

NOTES

TASTE

☐ TART
☐ BITTER
☐ SWEET
☐ BOOZY

NOTES

PALATE (THE WAY THE BEER FEELS IN YOUR MOUTH)

☐ LIGHT-BODIED (THIN + WATERY)
☐ MEDIUM-BODIED (LIGHT + FULL)
☐ FULL-BODIED (RICH + CREAMY)
☐ EFFERVESCENT

NOTES

BEER TASTING NOTES

COMPARISONS

FOOD/MEAL PAIRINGS

SHARED WITH (FAMILY/FRIENDS)

RECOMMEND?
☐ YES   ☐ NO

RATING
☐ 1   ☐ 2   ☐ 3   ☐ 4   ☐ 5   ☐ 6   ☐ 7   ☐ 8   ☐ 9   ☐ 10

SUMMARY

BEER TASTING NOTES

BEER NAME

BREWERY

TASTING DATE: **STYLE**

ALCOHOL BY VOLUME: **BOTTLED BY / BEST BY**   **PRICE**

CONTAINER
- ☐ BOTTLE
- ☐ CAN
- ☐ DRAFT
- ☐ GROWLER
- ☐ CASK
- ☐ OTHER

APPEARANCE
- ☐ GOLDEN
- ☐ AMBER
- ☐ COPPER
- ☐ RED
- ☐ BROWN
- ☐ BLACK
- ☐ OTHER

CLARITY
- ☐ CRYSTAL
- ☐ CLEAR
- ☐ HAZY
- ☐ OPAQUE
- ☐ OTHER

HEAD SIZE

HEAD RETENTION

HEAD DESCRIPTION
- ☐ SPARSE
- ☐ LIGHT
- ☐ CREAMY
- ☐ SOAPY
- ☐ FROTHY
- ☐ OTHER

SEDIMENT
- ☐ NONE
- ☐ SOME
- ☐ TONS

AROMA
- ☐ MALTY
- ☐ ROASTY
- ☐ HOPPY
- ☐ EARTHY
- ☐ FRUITY
- ☐ SOUR
- ☐ SPICY
- ☐ SMOKEY

NOTES

TASTE
- ☐ TART
- ☐ BITTER
- ☐ SWEET
- ☐ BOOZY

NOTES

PALATE (THE WAY THE BEER FEELS IN YOUR MOUTH)
- ☐ LIGHT-BODIED (THIN + WATERY)
- ☐ MEDIUM-BODIED (LIGHT + FULL)
- ☐ FULL-BODIED (RICH + CREAMY)
- ☐ EFFERVESCENT

NOTES

BEER TASTING NOTES

COMPARISONS

FOOD/MEAL PAIRINGS

SHARED WITH (FAMILY/FRIENDS)

RECOMMEND?
☐ YES ☐ NO

RATING
☐ 1 ☐ 2 ☐ 3 ☐ 4 ☐ 5 ☐ 6 ☐ 7 ☐ 8 ☐ 9 ☐ 10

SUMMARY

BEER TASTING NOTES

BEER NAME

BREWERY

TASTING DATE: **STYLE**

ALCOHOL BY VOLUME: **BOTTLED BY / BEST BY**   **PRICE**

CONTAINER
- ☐ BOTTLE
- ☐ CAN
- ☐ DRAFT
- ☐ GROWLER
- ☐ CASK
- ☐ OTHER

APPEARANCE
- ☐ GOLDEN
- ☐ AMBER
- ☐ COPPER
- ☐ RED
- ☐ BROWN
- ☐ BLACK
- ☐ OTHER

CLARITY
- ☐ CRYSTAL
- ☐ CLEAR
- ☐ HAZY
- ☐ OPAQUE
- ☐ OTHER

HEAD SIZE

HEAD RETENTION

HEAD DESCRIPTION
- ☐ SPARSE   ☐ OTHER
- ☐ LIGHT
- ☐ CREAMY
- ☐ SOAPY
- ☐ FROTHY

SEDIMENT
- ☐ NONE
- ☐ SOME
- ☐ TONS

AROMA
- ☐ MALTY
- ☐ ROASTY
- ☐ HOPPY
- ☐ EARTHY
- ☐ FRUITY
- ☐ SOUR
- ☐ SPICY
- ☐ SMOKEY

NOTES

TASTE
- ☐ TART
- ☐ BITTER
- ☐ SWEET
- ☐ BOOZY

NOTES

PALATE (THE WAY THE BEER FEELS IN YOUR MOUTH)
- ☐ LIGHT-BODIED (THIN + WATERY)
- ☐ MEDIUM-BODIED (LIGHT + FULL)
- ☐ FULL-BODIED (RICH + CREAMY)
- ☐ EFFERVESCENT

NOTES

BEER TASTING NOTES

COMPARISONS

FOOD/MEAL PAIRINGS

SHARED WITH (FAMILY/FRIENDS)

RECOMMEND?
☐ YES   ☐ NO

RATING
☐ 1   ☐ 2   ☐ 3   ☐ 4   ☐ 5   ☐ 6   ☐ 7   ☐ 8   ☐ 9   ☐ 10

SUMMARY

BEER TASTING NOTES

BEER NAME

BREWERY

TASTING DATE: **STYLE**

ALCOHOL BY VOLUME: **BOTTLED BY / BEST BY** **PRICE**

CONTAINER	APPEARANCE	CLARITY	HEAD SIZE	
☐ BOTTLE	☐ GOLDEN	☐ CRYSTAL	**HEAD RETENTION**	
☐ CAN	☐ AMBER	☐ CLEAR		
☐ DRAFT	☐ COPPER	☐ HAZY	**HEAD DESCRIPTION**	**SEDIMENT**
☐ GROWLER	☐ RED	☐ OPAQUE	☐ SPARSE ☐ OTHER	☐ NONE
☐ CASK	☐ BROWN	☐ OTHER	☐ LIGHT	☐ SOME
☐ OTHER	☐ BLACK		☐ CREAMY	☐ TONS
	☐ OTHER		☐ SOAPY	
			☐ FROTHY	

AROMA

☐ MALTY
☐ ROASTY
☐ HOPPY
☐ EARTHY
☐ FRUITY
☐ SOUR
☐ SPICY
☐ SMOKEY

NOTES

TASTE

☐ TART
☐ BITTER
☐ SWEET
☐ BOOZY

NOTES

PALATE (THE WAY THE BEER FEELS IN YOUR MOUTH)

☐ LIGHT-BODIED (THIN + WATERY)
☐ MEDIUM-BODIED (LIGHT + FULL)
☐ FULL-BODIED (RICH + CREAMY)
☐ EFFERVESCENT

NOTES

BEER TASTING NOTES

COMPARISONS

FOOD/MEAL PAIRINGS

SHARED WITH (FAMILY/FRIENDS)

RECOMMEND?
☐ YES ☐ NO

RATING
☐ 1 ☐ 2 ☐ 3 ☐ 4 ☐ 5 ☐ 6 ☐ 7 ☐ 8 ☐ 9 ☐ 10

SUMMARY

BEER TASTING NOTES

BEER NAME

BREWERY

TASTING DATE: STYLE

ALCOHOL BY VOLUME: BOTTLED BY / BEST BY   PRICE

CONTAINER
- ☐ BOTTLE
- ☐ CAN
- ☐ DRAFT
- ☐ GROWLER
- ☐ CASK
- ☐ OTHER

APPEARANCE
- ☐ GOLDEN
- ☐ AMBER
- ☐ COPPER
- ☐ RED
- ☐ BROWN
- ☐ BLACK
- ☐ OTHER

CLARITY
- ☐ CRYSTAL
- ☐ CLEAR
- ☐ HAZY
- ☐ OPAQUE
- ☐ OTHER

HEAD SIZE

HEAD RETENTION

HEAD DESCRIPTION
- ☐ SPARSE
- ☐ LIGHT
- ☐ CREAMY
- ☐ SOAPY
- ☐ FROTHY
- ☐ OTHER

SEDIMENT
- ☐ NONE
- ☐ SOME
- ☐ TONS

AROMA
- ☐ MALTY
- ☐ ROASTY
- ☐ HOPPY
- ☐ EARTHY
- ☐ FRUITY
- ☐ SOUR
- ☐ SPICY
- ☐ SMOKEY

NOTES

TASTE
- ☐ TART
- ☐ BITTER
- ☐ SWEET
- ☐ BOOZY

NOTES

PALATE (THE WAY THE BEER FEELS IN YOUR MOUTH)
- ☐ LIGHT-BODIED (THIN + WATERY)
- ☐ MEDIUM-BODIED (LIGHT + FULL)
- ☐ FULL-BODIED (RICH + CREAMY)
- ☐ EFFERVESCENT

NOTES

BEER TASTING NOTES

COMPARISONS

FOOD/MEAL PAIRINGS

SHARED WITH (FAMILY/FRIENDS)

RECOMMEND?   RATING
☐ YES ☐ NO   ☐ 1 ☐ 2 ☐ 3 ☐ 4 ☐ 5 ☐ 6 ☐ 7 ☐ 8 ☐ 9 ☐ 10

SUMMARY

BEER TASTING NOTES

BEER NAME

BREWERY

TASTING DATE: STYLE

ALCOHOL BY VOLUME: BOTTLED BY / BEST BY PRICE

CONTAINER
- [ ] BOTTLE
- [ ] CAN
- [ ] DRAFT
- [ ] GROWLER
- [ ] CASK
- [ ] OTHER

APPEARANCE
- [ ] GOLDEN
- [ ] AMBER
- [ ] COPPER
- [ ] RED
- [ ] BROWN
- [ ] BLACK
- [ ] OTHER

CLARITY
- [ ] CRYSTAL
- [ ] CLEAR
- [ ] HAZY
- [ ] OPAQUE
- [ ] OTHER

HEAD SIZE

HEAD RETENTION

HEAD DESCRIPTION
- [ ] SPARSE
- [ ] LIGHT
- [ ] CREAMY
- [ ] SOAPY
- [ ] FROTHY
- [ ] OTHER

SEDIMENT
- [ ] NONE
- [ ] SOME
- [ ] TONS

AROMA
- [ ] MALTY
- [ ] ROASTY
- [ ] HOPPY
- [ ] EARTHY
- [ ] FRUITY
- [ ] SOUR
- [ ] SPICY
- [ ] SMOKEY

NOTES

TASTE
- [ ] TART
- [ ] BITTER
- [ ] SWEET
- [ ] BOOZY

NOTES

PALATE (THE WAY THE BEER FEELS IN YOUR MOUTH)
- [ ] LIGHT-BODIED (THIN + WATERY)
- [ ] MEDIUM-BODIED (LIGHT + FULL)
- [ ] FULL-BODIED (RICH + CREAMY)
- [ ] EFFERVESCENT

NOTES

BEER TASTING NOTES

COMPARISONS

FOOD/MEAL PAIRINGS

SHARED WITH (FAMILY/FRIENDS)

RECOMMEND? ☐ YES ☐ NO

RATING ☐ 1 ☐ 2 ☐ 3 ☐ 4 ☐ 5 ☐ 6 ☐ 7 ☐ 8 ☐ 9 ☐ 10

SUMMARY

BEER TASTING NOTES

BEER NAME

BREWERY

TASTING DATE: **STYLE**

ALCOHOL BY VOLUME: **BOTTLED BY / BEST BY** **PRICE**

CONTAINER	APPEARANCE	CLARITY	HEAD SIZE	
			HEAD RETENTION	
☐ BOTTLE	☐ GOLDEN	☐ CRYSTAL		
☐ CAN	☐ AMBER	☐ CLEAR	**HEAD DESCRIPTION**	**SEDIMENT**
☐ DRAFT	☐ COPPER	☐ HAZY	☐ SPARSE ☐ OTHER	☐ NONE
☐ GROWLER	☐ RED	☐ OPAQUE	☐ LIGHT	☐ SOME
☐ CASK	☐ BROWN	☐ OTHER	☐ CREAMY	☐ TONS
☐ OTHER	☐ BLACK		☐ SOAPY	
	☐ OTHER		☐ FROTHY	

AROMA

☐ MALTY
☐ ROASTY
☐ HOPPY
☐ EARTHY
☐ FRUITY
☐ SOUR
☐ SPICY
☐ SMOKEY

NOTES

TASTE

☐ TART
☐ BITTER
☐ SWEET
☐ BOOZY

NOTES

PALATE (THE WAY THE BEER FEELS IN YOUR MOUTH)

☐ LIGHT-BODIED (THIN + WATERY)
☐ MEDIUM-BODIED (LIGHT + FULL)
☐ FULL-BODIED (RICH + CREAMY)
☐ EFFERVESCENT

NOTES

BEER TASTING NOTES

COMPARISONS

FOOD/MEAL PAIRINGS

SHARED WITH (FAMILY/FRIENDS)

RECOMMEND? ☐ YES ☐ NO

RATING ☐ 1 ☐ 2 ☐ 3 ☐ 4 ☐ 5 ☐ 6 ☐ 7 ☐ 8 ☐ 9 ☐ 10

SUMMARY

BEER TASTING NOTES

BEER NAME

BREWERY

TASTING DATE: STYLE

ALCOHOL BY VOLUME: BOTTLED BY / BEST BY PRICE

CONTAINER
- [ ] BOTTLE
- [ ] CAN
- [ ] DRAFT
- [ ] GROWLER
- [ ] CASK
- [ ] OTHER

APPEARANCE
- [ ] GOLDEN
- [ ] AMBER
- [ ] COPPER
- [ ] RED
- [ ] BROWN
- [ ] BLACK
- [ ] OTHER

CLARITY
- [ ] CRYSTAL
- [ ] CLEAR
- [ ] HAZY
- [ ] OPAQUE
- [ ] OTHER

HEAD SIZE

HEAD RETENTION

HEAD DESCRIPTION
- [ ] SPARSE
- [ ] LIGHT
- [ ] CREAMY
- [ ] SOAPY
- [ ] FROTHY
- [ ] OTHER

SEDIMENT
- [ ] NONE
- [ ] SOME
- [ ] TONS

AROMA
- [ ] MALTY
- [ ] ROASTY
- [ ] HOPPY
- [ ] EARTHY
- [ ] FRUITY
- [ ] SOUR
- [ ] SPICY
- [ ] SMOKEY

NOTES

TASTE
- [ ] TART
- [ ] BITTER
- [ ] SWEET
- [ ] BOOZY

NOTES

PALATE (THE WAY THE BEER FEELS IN YOUR MOUTH)
- [ ] LIGHT-BODIED (THIN + WATERY)
- [ ] MEDIUM-BODIED (LIGHT + FULL)
- [ ] FULL-BODIED (RICH + CREAMY)
- [ ] EFFERVESCENT

NOTES

BEER TASTING NOTES

COMPARISONS

FOOD/MEAL PAIRINGS

SHARED WITH (FAMILY/FRIENDS)

RECOMMEND?
☐ YES ☐ NO

RATING
☐ 1 ☐ 2 ☐ 3 ☐ 4 ☐ 5 ☐ 6 ☐ 7 ☐ 8 ☐ 9 ☐ 10

SUMMARY

BEER TASTING NOTES

BEER NAME

BREWERY

TASTING DATE: **STYLE**

ALCOHOL BY VOLUME: **BOTTLED BY / BEST BY**   **PRICE**

CONTAINER

- ☐ BOTTLE
- ☐ CAN
- ☐ DRAFT
- ☐ GROWLER
- ☐ CASK
- ☐ OTHER

APPEARANCE

- ☐ GOLDEN
- ☐ AMBER
- ☐ COPPER
- ☐ RED
- ☐ BROWN
- ☐ BLACK
- ☐ OTHER

CLARITY

- ☐ CRYSTAL
- ☐ CLEAR
- ☐ HAZY
- ☐ OPAQUE
- ☐ OTHER

HEAD SIZE

HEAD RETENTION

HEAD DESCRIPTION

- ☐ SPARSE
- ☐ OTHER
- ☐ LIGHT
- ☐ CREAMY
- ☐ SOAPY
- ☐ FROTHY

SEDIMENT

- ☐ NONE
- ☐ SOME
- ☐ TONS

AROMA

- ☐ MALTY
- ☐ ROASTY
- ☐ HOPPY
- ☐ EARTHY
- ☐ FRUITY
- ☐ SOUR
- ☐ SPICY
- ☐ SMOKEY

NOTES

TASTE

- ☐ TART
- ☐ BITTER
- ☐ SWEET
- ☐ BOOZY

NOTES

PALATE (THE WAY THE BEER FEELS IN YOUR MOUTH)

- ☐ LIGHT-BODIED (THIN + WATERY)
- ☐ MEDIUM-BODIED (LIGHT + FULL)
- ☐ FULL-BODIED (RICH + CREAMY)
- ☐ EFFERVESCENT

NOTES

BEER TASTING NOTES

COMPARISONS

FOOD/MEAL PAIRINGS

SHARED WITH (FAMILY/FRIENDS)

RECOMMEND?
☐ YES ☐ NO

RATING
☐ 1 ☐ 2 ☐ 3 ☐ 4 ☐ 5 ☐ 6 ☐ 7 ☐ 8 ☐ 9 ☐ 10

SUMMARY

BEER TASTING NOTES

BEER NAME

BREWERY

TASTING DATE: **STYLE**

ALCOHOL BY VOLUME: **BOTTLED BY / BEST BY** **PRICE**

CONTAINER	APPEARANCE	CLARITY	HEAD SIZE	
			HEAD RETENTION	
☐ BOTTLE	☐ GOLDEN	☐ CRYSTAL		
☐ CAN	☐ AMBER	☐ CLEAR	**HEAD DESCRIPTION**	**SEDIMENT**
☐ DRAFT	☐ COPPER	☐ HAZY	☐ SPARSE ☐ OTHER	☐ NONE
☐ GROWLER	☐ RED	☐ OPAQUE	☐ LIGHT	☐ SOME
☐ CASK	☐ BROWN	☐ OTHER	☐ CREAMY	☐ TONS
☐ OTHER	☐ BLACK		☐ SOAPY	
	☐ OTHER		☐ FROTHY	

AROMA

☐ MALTY
☐ ROASTY
☐ HOPPY
☐ EARTHY
☐ FRUITY
☐ SOUR
☐ SPICY
☐ SMOKEY

NOTES

TASTE

☐ TART
☐ BITTER
☐ SWEET
☐ BOOZY

NOTES

PALATE (THE WAY THE BEER FEELS IN YOUR MOUTH)

☐ LIGHT-BODIED (THIN + WATERY)
☐ MEDIUM-BODIED (LIGHT + FULL)
☐ FULL-BODIED (RICH + CREAMY)
☐ EFFERVESCENT

NOTES

BEER TASTING NOTES

COMPARISONS

FOOD/MEAL PAIRINGS

SHARED WITH (FAMILY/FRIENDS)

RECOMMEND? ☐ YES ☐ NO

RATING ☐1 ☐2 ☐3 ☐4 ☐5 ☐6 ☐7 ☐8 ☐9 ☐10

SUMMARY

BEER TASTING NOTES

BEER NAME

BREWERY

TASTING DATE: STYLE

ALCOHOL BY VOLUME: BOTTLED BY / BEST BY   PRICE

CONTAINER
- [ ] BOTTLE
- [ ] CAN
- [ ] DRAFT
- [ ] GROWLER
- [ ] CASK
- [ ] OTHER

APPEARANCE
- [ ] GOLDEN
- [ ] AMBER
- [ ] COPPER
- [ ] RED
- [ ] BROWN
- [ ] BLACK
- [ ] OTHER

CLARITY
- [ ] CRYSTAL
- [ ] CLEAR
- [ ] HAZY
- [ ] OPAQUE
- [ ] OTHER

HEAD SIZE

HEAD RETENTION

HEAD DESCRIPTION
- [ ] SPARSE
- [ ] LIGHT
- [ ] CREAMY
- [ ] SOAPY
- [ ] FROTHY
- [ ] OTHER

SEDIMENT
- [ ] NONE
- [ ] SOME
- [ ] TONS

AROMA
- [ ] MALTY
- [ ] ROASTY
- [ ] HOPPY
- [ ] EARTHY
- [ ] FRUITY
- [ ] SOUR
- [ ] SPICY
- [ ] SMOKEY

NOTES

TASTE
- [ ] TART
- [ ] BITTER
- [ ] SWEET
- [ ] BOOZY

NOTES

PALATE (THE WAY THE BEER FEELS IN YOUR MOUTH)
- [ ] LIGHT-BODIED (THIN + WATERY)
- [ ] MEDIUM-BODIED (LIGHT + FULL)
- [ ] FULL-BODIED (RICH + CREAMY)
- [ ] EFFERVESCENT

NOTES

BEER TASTING NOTES

COMPARISONS

FOOD/MEAL PAIRINGS

SHARED WITH (FAMILY/FRIENDS)

RECOMMEND? ☐ YES ☐ NO

RATING ☐ 1 ☐ 2 ☐ 3 ☐ 4 ☐ 5 ☐ 6 ☐ 7 ☐ 8 ☐ 9 ☐ 10

SUMMARY

BEER TASTING NOTES

BEER NAME

BREWERY

TASTING DATE: STYLE

ALCOHOL BY VOLUME: BOTTLED BY / BEST BY   PRICE

CONTAINER
- ☐ BOTTLE
- ☐ CAN
- ☐ DRAFT
- ☐ GROWLER
- ☐ CASK
- ☐ OTHER

APPEARANCE
- ☐ GOLDEN
- ☐ AMBER
- ☐ COPPER
- ☐ RED
- ☐ BROWN
- ☐ BLACK
- ☐ OTHER

CLARITY
- ☐ CRYSTAL
- ☐ CLEAR
- ☐ HAZY
- ☐ OPAQUE
- ☐ OTHER

HEAD SIZE

HEAD RETENTION

HEAD DESCRIPTION
- ☐ SPARSE   ☐ OTHER
- ☐ LIGHT
- ☐ CREAMY
- ☐ SOAPY
- ☐ FROTHY

SEDIMENT
- ☐ NONE
- ☐ SOME
- ☐ TONS

AROMA
- ☐ MALTY
- ☐ ROASTY
- ☐ HOPPY
- ☐ EARTHY
- ☐ FRUITY
- ☐ SOUR
- ☐ SPICY
- ☐ SMOKEY

NOTES

TASTE
- ☐ TART
- ☐ BITTER
- ☐ SWEET
- ☐ BOOZY

NOTES

PALATE (THE WAY THE BEER FEELS IN YOUR MOUTH)
- ☐ LIGHT-BODIED (THIN + WATERY)
- ☐ MEDIUM-BODIED (LIGHT + FULL)
- ☐ FULL-BODIED (RICH + CREAMY)
- ☐ EFFERVESCENT

NOTES

BEER TASTING NOTES

COMPARISONS

FOOD/MEAL PAIRINGS

SHARED WITH (FAMILY/FRIENDS)

RECOMMEND?
☐ YES   ☐ NO

RATING
☐ 1 ☐ 2 ☐ 3 ☐ 4 ☐ 5 ☐ 6 ☐ 7 ☐ 8 ☐ 9 ☐ 10

SUMMARY

FAVORITES

BEER NAME	DATE
BREWERY	STYLE

BEER NAME	DATE
BREWERY	STYLE

BEER NAME	DATE
BREWERY	STYLE

BEER NAME	DATE
BREWERY	STYLE

BEER NAME	DATE
BREWERY	STYLE

BEER NAME	DATE
BREWERY	STYLE

BEER NAME	DATE
BREWERY	STYLE

BEER NAME	DATE
BREWERY	STYLE

BEER NAME	DATE
BREWERY	STYLE

FAVORITES

BEER NAME		DATE	
BREWERY		STYLE	
BEER NAME		DATE	
BREWERY		STYLE	
BEER NAME		DATE	
BREWERY		STYLE	
BEER NAME		DATE	
BREWERY		STYLE	
BEER NAME		DATE	
BREWERY		STYLE	
BEER NAME		DATE	
BREWERY		STYLE	
BEER NAME		DATE	
BREWERY		STYLE	
BEER NAME		DATE	
BREWERY		STYLE	
BEER NAME		DATE	
BREWERY		STYLE	

FAVORITES

BEER NAME		DATE	
BREWERY		STYLE	

BEER NAME		DATE	
BREWERY		STYLE	

BEER NAME		DATE	
BREWERY		STYLE	

BEER NAME		DATE	
BREWERY		STYLE	

BEER NAME		DATE	
BREWERY		STYLE	

BEER NAME		DATE	
BREWERY		STYLE	

BEER NAME		DATE	
BREWERY		STYLE	

BEER NAME		DATE	
BREWERY		STYLE	

BEER NAME		DATE	
BREWERY		STYLE	

FAVORITES

BEER NAME	DATE
BREWERY	STYLE

BEER NAME	DATE
BREWERY	STYLE

BEER NAME	DATE
BREWERY	STYLE

BEER NAME	DATE
BREWERY	STYLE

BEER NAME	DATE
BREWERY	STYLE

BEER NAME	DATE
BREWERY	STYLE

BEER NAME	DATE
BREWERY	STYLE

BEER NAME	DATE
BREWERY	STYLE

BEER NAME	DATE
BREWERY	STYLE

FAVORITES

BEER NAME		DATE	
BREWERY		STYLE	
BEER NAME		DATE	
BREWERY		STYLE	
BEER NAME		DATE	
BREWERY		STYLE	
BEER NAME		DATE	
BREWERY		STYLE	
BEER NAME		DATE	
BREWERY		STYLE	
BEER NAME		DATE	
BREWERY		STYLE	
BEER NAME		DATE	
BREWERY		STYLE	
BEER NAME		DATE	
BREWERY		STYLE	
BEER NAME		DATE	
BREWERY		STYLE	

www.ingramcontent.com/pod-product-compliance
Lightning Source LLC
Chambersburg PA
CBHW071407080526
44587CB00017B/3201